PULL MY FINGER!

NORMA HUNTER

Pull My Finger
Story by Norma Hunter
Illustrations by Ben Crane

© 2024 Norma Hunter

No part of this publication may be reproduced in whole or in part, stored in a retrieval system, or transmitted in any form or by any means, electronic, mechanical, photocopying, recording, or otherwise, without written permission from the publisher. For information regarding permission, write to Norma Hunter, Box 1508, Shaunavon, SK S0N 2M0

ISBN: 979-8-3448-9709-7

He breaks Nannie's rules, he snores, he licks his plate,
and plays an amazing tuba – out his behind –
all to the tune of laughter (with life lessons thrown in)!
Who knew that being married to a Papa could be so much fun?

I love that I live my life on the farm
    It holds tons of memories and plenty of charm.

    But I love it best when Papa is there
        There's something he does that's a hoot anywhere.

We go on the Rhino ... he lets me steer
Sometimes he does it
when we're in the clear.

We chase round the shop
with the bikes and go karts,
Often that's where
all the craziness starts.

Sometimes he swings me
like I am a rocket,
Yahoo! We're a real live
swing-handle and socket!

I scream when he tosses me
up in the sky.
IT happens so easy...

... like he doesn't try!

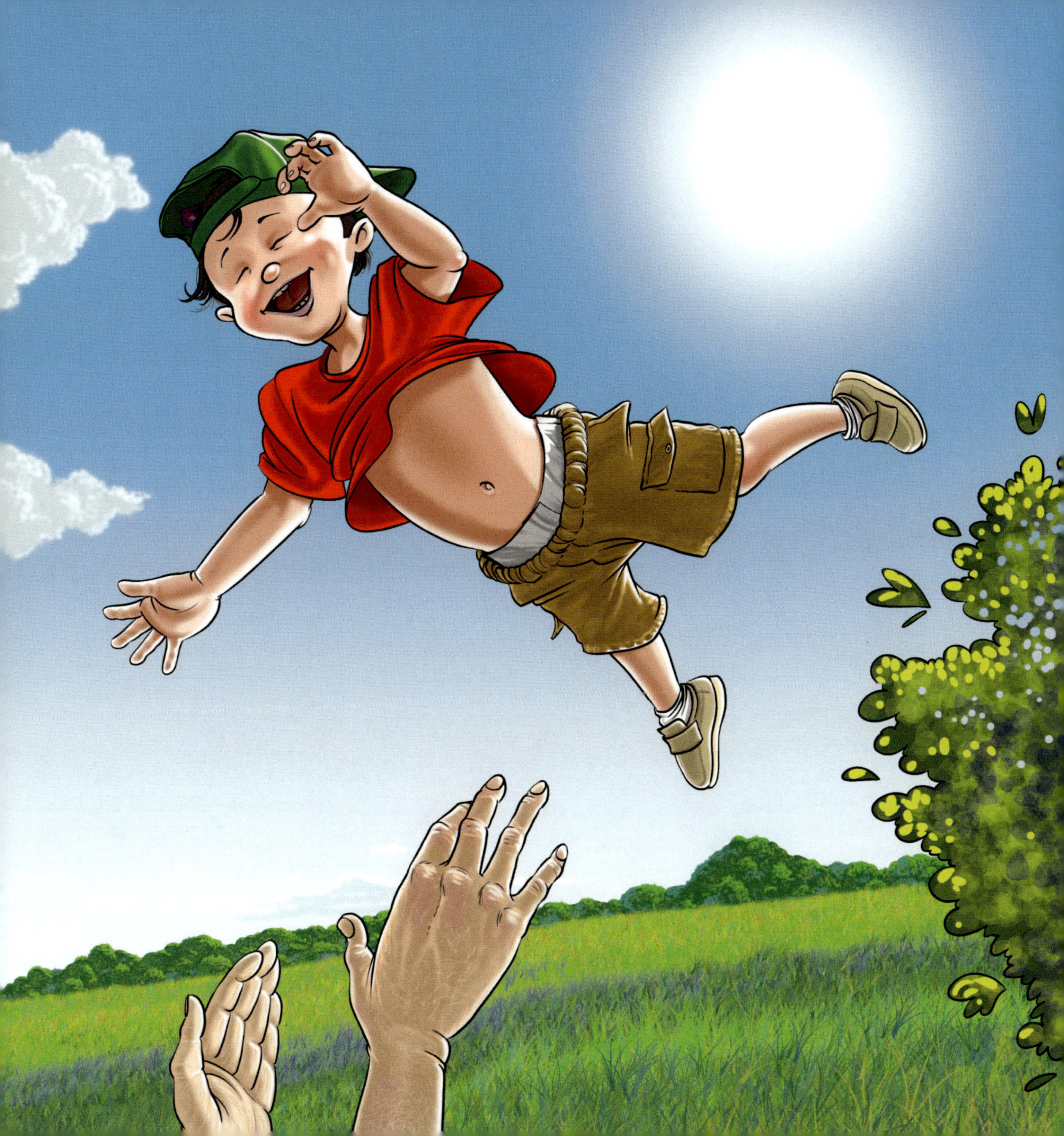

He spins me around
the floor 'til I'm dizzy,
Then sometimes he does **IT**
and I'm in a tizzy!

He hides yummy treats
for us to go find,
Then says **IT** - I roar
and check his behind.

We play hide and seek
all over the house,
And when Papa hides
he's just like a mouse.

Then when he swings me up high in a towel,
We flip round and then-
he says **IT**
   with a growl!

We cuddle up close
and he holds me real tight.
I feel safe and I'd like
to stay there all night.

But when he whispers right into my hair, "Just pull my finger" I know that **it's** there!

Then I start to giggle
and know time will tell...
And I hear that sound
and I smell that smell!
Once in awhile the bad smell
it will linger,
But it's worth it all when he says
"Pull my finger!"

I pull really hard
   and I wait for the rumbly
It comes down below...
right from his tumbly.

It jiggles the couch where we sit -
   that's no joke.
   Sometimes the smell makes me
      think that I'll choke!

I cough and I spit
and I hork and I gag.
Then giggle and roll,
and I snort and I sag.

The laughter, it starts way down from my toes,
As that gross smell rises right up to my nose.

The shrieking, it follows
the smell like a race!
I laugh 'til the tears
just roll down my face.

And just when I think that the laughter will end I say "Oh Papa - please do it again!"

It NEVER works
when I pull Papa's feet,
Or his ankles, or legs,
or his ears or his cheek.

If I yank on his pinky
or pull on his thumb,
Nothing - **NO NOTHING** -
comes out of Pop's bum!

Oh he is so funny
 I laugh 'til I snort,
  My insides start hurting,
   my breathing is short.

Sometimes the giggles start
 down at my toes,
  then bubble right up
   and come out my nose!

They rumble and tumble
inside my tummy -
and sometimes they're sneaky
and slip out
MY BUMMY!

Manufactured by Amazon.ca
Bolton, ON